Beginning
Wing Chun Kuen
By Hendrik Santo

Edited by Robert Chu

Revision 1.3

6 13 3 Publications

Beginning
Wing Chun Kuen

咏春 6.13.3

Dedication

To the peacemakers of the past, present, and future.

"I wish now to achieve the result and become an honored king, who then returns to save as many beings as there are sand grains in the Ganges. I offer this deep thought to those who are as countless as the motes of dust of the Buddhalands, To repay the kindness shown me by the Buddha."

- *Shurangama Sutra*

Disclaimer

Please note that the author and publisher of this book are NOT RESPONSIBLE in any manner whatsoever for any injury that may result from practicing the techniques and/or following the instructions given within. Since the physical activities described herein may be too strenuous in nature for some readers to engage in safely, it is essential that a physician be consulted prior to training.

Table of Contents

Editor's Preface

I am delighted to work with my Yik Kam Wing Chun Kuen Sifu, Hendrik Santo, in the release of his third book, **Beginning Wing Chun Kuen.**

As the focus of martial arts has been a major driving force in my life, I was fascinated with an older version of Wing Chun Kuen. To date, I have delved deeply into several lineages, including the Yip Man (aka Ip Man) lineage from Hawkins Cheung, Yuen Kay Shan, Gu Lao, Law Family Sae Hoc Wing Chun, and the iYik Kam Wing Chun Educational Platform system. I have practiced Wing Chun Kuen for over forty years and have written many articles, and been the subject of many articles and videos on the subject. As history was one of my interests, I delved into the past and research almost all lineages of Wing Chun.

In compiling information for "Complete Wing Chun, The Definitive Guide to Wing Chun's History and Traditions" which I co-authored in 1998, I found an old interview of Ip Man in the Hong Kong based **New Martial Hero** magazine in 1972. Recently, I shared the article with Hendrik, along with many of the *Kuen Kuit* found in the Yip Man and Yuen Kay Shan systems. Knowing Hendrik's process of 6 13 3, as described in the book, *"Basic Ancient Wing Chun Kuen Art and Science"* allowed me to analyze the elements in the interview and make comparisons to today's Wing Chun Kuen practice.
⁇

Training in 6 13 3 made me realize modern day Wing Chun Kuen practices are taught differently than in old Wing Chun Kuen. For example, many of the prized body structure methods in Wing Chun Kuen are really Long Fist methods. In structure, there is a lot of holding tension in the body in these methods. Although it seems strong, it is not full potential, when just holding tension. Holding is stagnant, inflexible, unhealthy, and unrelaxed. Furthermore, breathing is shallow in this method. Because you are breathing with the chest, one runs out of wind faster. Without being relaxed, stagnation is in the body.

Instead of holding on to it, one needs to let holding structure go and relax, and keep the body loose. This allows Qi and blood to flow, and heal the body. If the body is loose, and the breathing is deep, the mind is calm and blissful. We can contrast this with the aggressive mindset of today's Wing Chun Kuen practitioners. If you face an opponent in a calm and blissful state, you can become more aware, rather than putting your mind in a highly charged emotional state in which you may overreact and have dangerous circumstances to deal with. Of course, the implications in daily life are unlimited if the mind is quiet and calm, and one can go back to deep breathing, and charge your body throughout the day.

If the mind is too aggressive, you are apt to have conflict with difficult people. With the correct Wing Chun Kuen mindset, you realize you can't change them, and arguing has no resolution, only creating more resentment and confusion, so in the calmness, one simply learns to disengage. People can be difficult through ignorance, stupidity, wanting to be the smartest, or right, and instead of dealing with it egotistically, just letting things go is best, as the anger and stress drain one's energy away. If one looks at the movie Ip Man, one can see how calm he is, even in stressful situations, and doesn't overreact.

Holding a structure is opposite of the methods of the Body Element of 6 13 3. Wing Chun Kuen is supposed to have a loose flexible body that even Grandmaster Ip Man stated in his 1972 interview, that the "body is like rattan". Although some speculate the article is counterfeit and suspect, the knowledge embodied in the article is not false. This "rattan body" quality is what we develop through the seven bows of the body – the feet bow, ankle bow, knee bow, hip bow, shoulder bow, elbow bow, and wrist bow. Having the flexibility in all the joints, where the body is not held rigidly, is the central idea. This does not mean being limp or lifeless, but rather alive and in the moment. This rattan analogy (which has been translated erroneously as "bamboo") also refers to the hands of Wing Chun Kuen: *Tan, Bong,* and *Fuk*. The interview states, "when the opponent strikes close, if one uses *Tan Sao, Fuk Sao,* or *Bong Sao* to receive the attack, that actual strike will be as if hitting on a rattan stick – one's defense will, at that moment of attack, become pushed back as a result of the force, just like rattan."

In Ip Man's 1972 interview, he describes Wing Chun Kuen as being the "Southern region, Stick to the Body, Short Strike, narrow stance, short bridges method." Today's Wing Chun Kuen, has maintained a greater distance than what Ip Man described, becoming a long range art. Many are trying to strike out and keep the opponent at bay. We can even note that there is a great change in stance, as the *Yee Ji Kim Yeung Ma* is described in that article as, "One fixates itself to the ground by spreading legs to a bit less than shoulder width and then sits down on an "invisible chair". Many of today's Wing Chun Kuen people have widened the base of the stances of *Yee Ji Kim Yeung Ma* and the *Chum Kiu Ma*.

What is known today in Wing Chun Kuen as *Yee Ji Kim Yeung Ma* 二字钳羊馬 has its origins in the *Ping Jian Dang* 平肩襠 of *Emei 12 Zhuang*. *Ping Jian Dang* is translated as Equal Shoulder Stance in English, but if we analyze the characters, it is composed of 3 characters - *Ping*, meaning "level" or "equal", or "even"; *Jian*, referring to the "shoulders", *Dang*, referring to the "crotch", implying the space between the legs, or "stance". Altogether, it is a stance with the width of the shoulders from top to bottom.

Ping Jian Dang is also known as *Yee Ji Kim Yeung Ma* with different characters - 二字钳陽馬– which can be translated in English as the "Parallel (legs) clamping/pinching of the Yang Channels"。 To the untrained ear, they sound almost alike, but the ramifications are quite evident here in this book. With the Ancient Wing Chun stance of the 1840's, breathing is more relaxed and deeper when toes are out, and if you are open, loose, light, then Qi and blood flows easier.

If your physical is primed, you have better awareness, and can better use action/reaction force flow with the relaxed sensitivity.

Even the punch described in the 1972 article is described by Ip Man, "The force exerted should be exactly like the way one strikes a hammer into the wall. Everyone who has used a hammer to hit a nail knows that if you struck it with brute force, not only does the nail fail to penetrate the wall, it might actually become deformed. One must strike the nail cautiously, using the wrist as an axis and lightly hammering it in. This is what Wing Chun is all about." Many of today's Wing Chun Kuen practitioners exert great forces with momentum in a distance to strike harder than is necessary. Perhaps we need to strike more carefully, targeting and selecting where we want to strike and minimizing the use of brute force, but utilizing controlled strength to strike the opponent.

So since 1972, Wing Chun Kuen has further degenerated into a long bridge striking art, using wide stances and brute force. One can wonder, *is what we're practicing even Wing Chun Kuen?*

In this work, you will have experienced Hendrik's more than 40 years of research to improve not only your Wing Chun Kuen, but to also address areas where you can be a balanced human being. Although I have studied other forms of Wing Chun, most have turned out to be unbalanced, preferring to focus as a weapon of self-defense. They have paled in comparison to iYik Kam Wing Chun Kuen Educational Platform as a holistic art balancing mind, body, and spirit.

You will read in the chapters that follow how Yip Man's article embraces the common data points of all Wing Chun, and is a legacy to be preserved, and shares in common all the points of old Wing Chun that seems to be forgotten by today's practitioners!

Author's Preface

The first goal of writing this book is to introduce the basics of Wing Chun Kuen, a "sticking body short strike" 貼身短打 art in a comprehensive, scientific, and systematic way. In this way, one will be able to study Wing Chun Kuen in an effective and efficient way, and also be able to understand what is the ancient design of Wing Chun Kuen in a simple and clear way.

The second goal of writing this book is to introduce Wing Chun Kuen to university educators, to make it possible for Wing Chun Kuen to become a formal education in Asian or Chinese arts study.

This book is built on top of the platform of my book - *Basic Ancient Wing Chun Kuen Science and Art*. These two books cover the major fundamentals of Wing Chun Kuen.

They are intended to be used as the textbooks for a semester class in a college or university to cover the science and art of Wing Chun Kuen study, or serve as the textbooks for other Asian formal martial art study.

Finally, I would like to express my deep appreciation to Sifu Robert Chu who made this book possible, and to Jack Chang and Trish Lowe for their generous help on modeling for the photos for this book.

September 30, 2016
Jakarta, Indonesia

Go tell the world I'm still around
I didn't fly, I'm coming down

Waiting up in heaven
I was never far from you
Spinning down I felt your every move

I Walk Alone, by Tarja

Introduction

Fighting is the thought of victory and defeat
It contradicts to the Way of enlightenment
Giving rise to the mind of four marks
How can one obtain Samadhi with fighting?

---- Sixth Patriarch Platform Sutra

The goal of this book is to introduce the basic core of the art of Wing Chun Kuen for educational purposes. The intention is to promote a scientific understanding in the art of Wing Chun Kuen so that quality Wing Chun Kuen skill can be developed; and to share the beauty of this fine art, to be appreciated. Furthermore, a scientific understanding prevents misleading and generalizing judgments, based on superficial information. This book is also intended to be a reference book and or a textbook, which can be used in formal college classroom.

Wu Shu (武術) is generally translated as "martial art", but it actually means the "technology to stop fighting", since the Chinese character Wu (武) means "stop fighting".

This book is intended for peaceful education. It is not intended to be a book of chasing for the number one best fighter or violence; instead the goal is to strengthen the body and self-defense.

The content of this book is based on tangible records of both Wing Chun Kuen and traditional Chinese martial arts. This book is arranged in a systematic way to present both the big picture and details, and comes with exercises or observations to experiment with for a better comprehension.

Finally, unless one has in depth experience in Wing Chun Kuen, it is strongly advised for one to study this book as one would study a completely new subject from the start; one needs to digest every detail before proceeding, as simply reading and speculating with one's mindset, without taking the time to digest, will not teach you much of the Wing Chun Kuen technology present in this book. In fact, it is very likely to cause misunderstanding.

Chapter One - What is Wing Chun Kuen?

IT IS CERTAIN THAT THESE WORDS EXPRESS THE TRUE VEHICLE,
WHOEVER DOES NOT ACCEPT THEM MAY INQUIRE AS THEY WISH.
IT CUTS DIRECTLY THROUGH TO THE SOURCE;
IT IS SEALED BY ALL BUDDHA.
I CANNOT PLUCK LEAVES AND SEEK OUT BRANCHES.

---Song of Enlightenment

According to traditional Chinese martial arts history, Wing Chun Kuen is a type of Southern Chinese martial art. The characteristics of Wing Chun Kuen is: stick to the body and short striking (贴身短打), short bridge and narrow stance (短桥窄马)、keen in short distance striking (or inch striking) (善發寸勁), and "accept the incoming, escort the leaving, when disengaged, thrust forward " (来留去送脱手直衝).

In order to understand accurately on the meaning of the above Wing Chun Kuen characteristics, one first needs to have a technical background in the Traditional Chinese martial arts.

The Long Fist art and the Short Strike art

According to the well- known Ming dynasty General Qi Jiguang (戚继光) who documented his ideas and practical experience in the book on military strategy - *Ji Xiao Xin Shu* (紀效新書), the traditional Chinese martial arts in the era of 1560 that stood out was classified into two distinct types of art, and they are the "Long Fist" and the "Short Strike". Short Strike (短打) is also named as "sticking to the body Short Strike" (貼身短打). Short Strike is also referred to as the "short bridge method" (短橋法), whereas Long Fist referred to as the "long bridge method" (長橋法).

The characteristics of Long Fist is that it is a dynamic, mobile art with fully extended arm or leg techniques; Long Fist always keeps a distance from its opponent for execution space, due to its mechanical design.

On the other hand, Short Strike has a characteristic of using a retracting arm to receive the incoming attack while closing in, and sticking to the opponent's body, to fight in "body to body" sticking range; uses retracting arm snapping strikes, elbows, combined with trips and throws as primary techniques.

Due to the differences of these two arts, the concept of fighting, the strategy of fighting, the use of strength in fighting, and body conditioning to support these arts are different.

The characteristics of the Long Fist art and the Short Strike art are as the following:

The advantage of Long Fist art is that the postures of the art are big, it can strike from long distance, and a larger posture yields a big motion. Under the same speed, bigger motion means a slower movement, and with big postures, the steps will be wider, and lead to difficulty in handling the center of gravity changes and therefore, be less agile.

In Long Fist, the arm will be extended straight, and as such, it reduces flexibility. Because the arm is extended, it is more difficult to change, and certain parts of the body are unprotected due to stretching out the limb. Long Fist also has a tendency of instability, if the motion is over shot.

In Short Strike, the posture is small, the motions are small, and utilizes a narrow stance, short bridge, with emphasis on agility; the body is well protected, and suitable to close in for short distance attacks with destructive strikes.

On the contrary, Long Fist is not suitable for close range fighting due to its naturally less protective guard. The fundamental idea of the Short Strike is "close in, stick to the opponent's body for destructive continuous chain strikes and/or takedown".

The figures below are a summary of Long Fist and Short Strike:

Figure 1 Long Fist and Short Strike

Long Fist art
Move forward/backward with arm extend outward, keep an execution distance

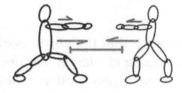

Short strike art
Arm retract, close in, keep a balance center axis

Figure 1A - Long Fist

Figure 1B   Short Strike

The Way of Wing Chun Kuen

The Way of Wing Chun Kuen is a variation of the way of Short Strike because it was designed with the Short Strike platform. The following is a Short Strike teaching by Zhang Heng Chiu (张横秋) in the early 1700's. This important writing describes the core basics of the Short Strike art.

The writing says:

"Long comes short accepts habitually closing in" (長來短接慣入身),
"Closing in takedown is surprisingly stunning" (入身趺撥好驚人),
"Inward wrapping open up left and right corner" (里裹打開左右角),
"Outward wrapping strike in searching within the chest" (外裹打入窩裡尋).

The first sentence of this writing, "Long comes short accepts habitually closing in" (長來短接慣入身), is the strategy and tactic of the Short Strike art. Since Wing Chun Kuen is a Short Strike art, this sentence is in fact, parallel to and supports the Wing Chun Kuen saying, "Accept what is incoming, escort what is leaving, when disengaged, thrust forward (來留去送脫手直衝)". This sentence serves as another data point to further verify and understand Wing Chun Kuen.

"Long comes, short receives, habitually close in to the opponent's body" (長來短接慣入身) is interpreted as the following, "Long coming", refers to a Long Fist attack with Long Fist mechanics; "Short receiving", means receiving the incoming attack with Short Strike mechanics; "Close in to the opponent's body", means to get close in to the opponent's body, as closing in to body sticking range; "Habitually close in to the opponent's body", means closing in to the opponent's body is needs to become a second nature for Short Strike practitioners.

Knowing the above multiple data points is similar to solving system equations. The Wing Chun Kuen saying, "Accept the incoming, escort what is leaving, when disengaged, thrust forward" (来留去送脱手直衝). "Accept the incoming" means "to receive"; "when disengaged, thrust forward" means "to close in", and, "Accepting the incoming, escort the leaving" means "to stick".

Thus, the Wing Chun Kuen saying means to "receive, stick, close in to the opponent's body", which fits the signature of the Short Strike art; with Wing Chun Kuen, one has to "Stick" or "Chi" (as in *Chi Sao*). Furthermore, the Wing Chun Kuen saying, "receive, close in, and attack are concurrent" (連消帶打, 打手即是消手) means that is different from other arts of dissolving, deflecting, or blocking before striking.

Figure 1.2 is a summary of the sticking to the body Short Strike Wing Chun Kuen.

Figure 1.3 shows a Short Strike art counter a Long Fist art.

Figure 1.4 shows a sample of Wing Chun Kuen technique in the sticking to the body range

Short strike receive and close in in concurrent

長來短接慣入身
Long come short receive habitully close in to the opponent's body

來留去送脱手直衝
Accept the incoming, escort the leaving, disengage thrust forward

Accept = Receive

Receive, Accept, Escort = stick = Chi as in Chi Sao

Disengage thrust forward = Close in to the opponent's body

Figure 1.2, the Sticking to the Body Short Strike Wing Chun Kuen concept

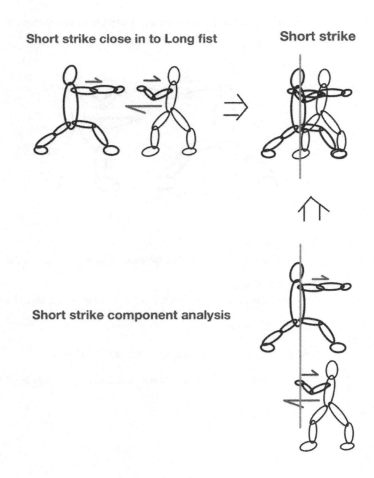

Figure 1.3 Short Strike counters Long Fist

24

Figure 1.4 Wing Chun Kuen in Sticking to the Body range

From these examples above, we can see that Wing Chun Kuen is based on receiving and sticking, instead of blocking, countering, or being against, resisting, or sustaining. The way of Wing Chun Kuen is to receive/stick, and at the same time, close in to the opponent's body. The way of receive/ stick and close in to the opponent is the signature of a flexible (柔) art, or soft art, or feminine art, which is the way of the sticking to the body and short striking. (貼身短打).

Note that the soft of Wing Chun refers to the Short Strike way of fighting strategy and momentum handling; it is not the *Tai Ji Quan* soft way, soft *Jin* (power), push hand, or soft practice of a set.

In addition, Wing Chun Kuen is not staying at a fixed location to block, withstand, or press forward; Wing Chun Kuen is also not moving backwards, moving away, or moving sideways to keep distance.

Chapter Two - The How of Wing Chun Kuen

THE ALMS-BOWL SUBDUE THE DRAGONS;
THE TIN STAFF VANQUISHES TIGERS,
AND THE GOLDEN RINGS OF ITS TWO PARTS SOUND IN CLEAR
SUCCESSION.
IT IS NO SYMBOLIC FORM UNSUPPORTED BY REAL EVENTS;
IT IS THE JEWELED STAFF OF THE BUDDHA, WHICH HE HIMSELF
PASSED DOWN.

---- *Song of Enlightenment*

In order to develop the skill of Wing Chun Kuen, one must know the What, Why, and How of Wing Chun Kuen. Since Wing Chun Kuen is a martial art based on physical momentum and strength exchange in a physical world, investigating the mechanics of the Short Strike is a must.

The Mechanics of Wing Chun Kuen

A good martial art is designed which makes use of the laws of physics, instead of relying fully upon muscular strength, which is subject to aging and changing daily; or some sort of mysterious internal power, which no one knows if it exists. Everything that exists in the physical realm has to be based on the law of physics. The design of Wing Chun Kuen is based on the law of physics, biomechanics, and *Yellow Emperor Classic of Chinese Medicine*. Wing Chun Kuen has a solid physical platform for it to be repeatable and duplicable, with quality. Thus, It is extremely critical to clearly understand the components of the Sticking to the Body Short Strike Wing Chun Kuen in order to make it work.

The core of the Wing Chun Kuen design is in its mechanical advantage using the lever system, and mechanical advantage of using torque. As in figure 2.1, a short load arm, or short bridge, has a mechanical advantage compared with the long load arm, or long bridge.

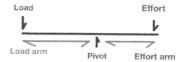

Mechanical advantage = Effort arm / Load arm

Effort = (Load X Load arm) / Effort arm

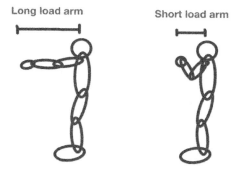

It takes less effort to handle the same load
with a short load arm

Figure 2.1 shows the mechanical advantage mechanism of Wing
Chun Kuen

As in figure 2.1A, Wing Chun Kuen, the Sticking to the Body Short Strike art, or Short Bridge art, is created based on the torque advantage of the short lever arm, or a position close to the axis of rotation, supporting an effective force handling.

Figure 2.1B sums up the mechanical advantage and torque advantage of Wing Chun Kuen. This is the basis of how less effort can handle larger incoming force, with the Wing Chun Kuen practitioner taking the position of the revolving door, keeping the opponent as close as possible.   A small spin in the center axis of the Wing Chun Kuen practitioner generates a big force on the opponent's side. A big force originating from the opponent can be handled with a small spin of the Wing Chun Kuen practitioner's center axis.

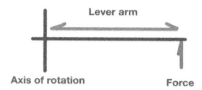

Lever arm

Axis of rotation

Force

Torque = Lever arm X Force

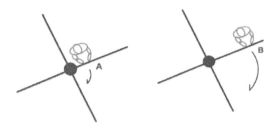

Torque advantage:

More force is needed to move the revolving door at point A compare with point B

More force is needed to stop the revolving door at point A compare with point B

Figure 2.1A shows the torque advantage mechanism of Wing Chun Kuen

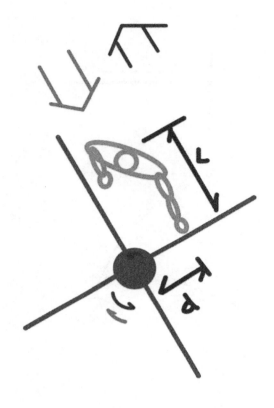

Figure 2.1B shows the mechanical design of Wing Chun Kuen.

In addition to the mechanical and torque advantage, the most effective power handling of the human arm is when the arm in action is positioned close to the center of gravity, or waist area. Thus, when dealing with a large power, the closer the arm resides to the waist area, the higher the effectiveness of the handling. In contrast, the further the arm extended outward from the waist area, the less effective the handling will be.

The Wing Chun Kuen concept of the "Hand resides in the center; Fist is issued from heart" (手留中, 拳從心發) are designed based on these above scientific considerations. In conclusion, these effective mechanical designs are the fundamentals of Wing Chun Kuen's "Keen in short power" (善發短勁) or using less effort to handle or overcome the stronger opponent. This is all based on physics and biomechanics, without myth.

In addition to the above mechanical and torque advantage, the Sticking to the body, Short Strike Wing Chun Kuen is a body sticking, body contact range fighting; this fighting range has a short launch to arrival time, that is, causing difficulty for the opponent to respond and to protect, or guard. Also, Sticking to the body, Short Strike also means to carry out a disruptive attack towards the opponent's center of gravity, or core; while jamming, sealing off, or disabling the opponent's limb. One torques the opponent's body while sticking to dissolve resistance and avoid getting tangled. This makes the attack more effective, and if intended, could be very destructive.

Furthermore, in order to implement the Sticking to the Body Short Strike art, one must avoid force against force confrontation, such as: resisting, blocking, or power struggling, at the Long Fist art range; for those types of actions will cause one to be tangled, tied up, or destroyed at Long Fist range.

Whether in attack or counter attack situations, while facing resistance from an opponent, one must retract the arm, while moving the body forward, instead of extending the arm to try to push the opponent outward.

The following Kuen Kuit are a description of Stick to the Body Short Strike Wing Chun Kuen 1840 at the sticking body range: *"Biu Jee* is poison, use it at emergency" (標指狠毒急可用); "Enemy is strong, while I am weak, using seal throat hand" (敵強孤弱封喉手); Tearing hands is for breaking the long bridge (撕手能破長橋法). Note that one must be using a "Sticking to the Body Short Strike" mind set to read these, or else if one is using a "Long Fist" mind set, one will completely miss the point.

In conclusion, the way of the Sticking to the Body Short Strike Wing Chun Kuen is to rapidly close in, stick to the opponent's body, while concurrently directly attacking the target, be it a strike or a takedown.

Long Fist and Short Strike power

Due to the natural differences of the Long Fist art and Short Strike art, certain power or strength generation methods fit one art better than the other art. The long strength fits Long Fist, while short strength fits Short Strike better.

In figure 2.3A, typical mechanics of generating long strength is moving the Center of gravity, or pushing/rotating the *Dan Tian*. This type of long strength or long power generates a powerful strike or high momentum strike, which pushes away the target object. In figure 2.3B, the mechanics of generating short strength is torque of the body, and/or the snapping action of the joints. This type of power generation generates a sharp strike or impulse strike. The snapping action creates the velocity for high impact without pushing the target object much. Due to the Sticking to the Body Short Strike range constraints, sharp impulse striking fits well into this type of art. It would be clumsy and ineffective to use a long strength type in a Short Strike art. Thus, the Wing Chun Kuen sun punch is a snapping strike with short power, which is inserted into the target like a nail, instead of a power strike of hitting with a swing of a heavy hammer.

Figure 2.3A, the long power/strength generation

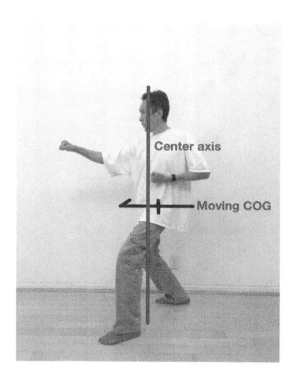

Figure 2.3B, the short power/strength generation

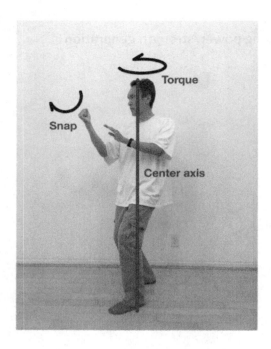

Body type force flow type power handling

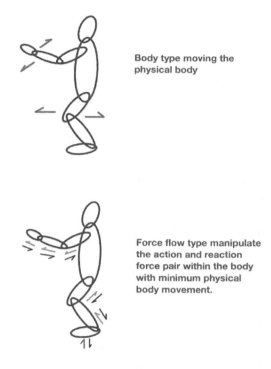

Body type moving the physical body

Force flow type manipulate the action and reaction force pair within the body with minimum physical body movement.

Figure 2.4, body type and force flow type of power handling

As in figure 2.4, to generate the body type of power, one needs to move the physical body. An example of body type power is the long strength - this is a great fit for the Long Fist in art in general.

Snapping and torque are also body type of power generation with less physical movement. While the force flow type of power, or strength handling, is a must for Short Strike when it is operating in the Body to Body sticking range, which requires instantaneous response.

Force flow type of strength handling is to handle the action/reaction force pair within the body, instead of moving the body parts, while ignoring the action/reaction force pair.

Furthermore, the sensing of strength in Wing Chun Kuen is a force flow play where one "listens" to the action/reaction force of the opponent; be it in friendly Chi Sau practice or a real Sticking to the Body range fighting. Details of body type and force flow type strength/power handling can be found in the book "*Basic Ancient Wing Chun Kuen Art and Science*" by Hendrik Santo.

Center Axis and Line of Attack

Center Axis is critical for the Short Strike art because it is the target which needs to be captured or destroyed as soon as possible; and it is the core of one's power generation for torque generation. Thus, the idea is one target to destroy the opponents' center axis, and concurrently, one making use of the one's center axis for the required torque generation.

As shown in figure 2.5, the "Line of Attack" is defined as the line which the opponent's both arms can strike or attack without having to move the opponent's body on a large scale. Thus, the name of the game is one does not want to be within the line of attack of the opponent, however, one wants the opponent to be within one's line of attack as shown in figure 2.5B. That way, one can safely close in to the opponent's body or attack.

It is a requirement for Short Strike art to track the opponent's center axis at all times for effective handling of the opponent's, and track the opponent's line of attack at all times to stay out of the attack zone. Due to these reasons, a Short Strike artist will face the opponent's center axis all the time, or face the opponent's shape (朝形对敌, 朝面追形); one simply tracks and looks at the opponent's central axis at every instant regardless of angle and movement dynamic.

Be able to absorb incoming forces at close range is analogous to a rattan vine. One is not an iron wall. One must not walk into the line of attack carelessly or blindly. It is predictable that fighting within the line of fire where both parties can strike each other is a power struggle, as shown in figure 2.5A; both parties are to trade strikes, as both parties will get hit, and the stronger and faster party will win.

Figure 2.5

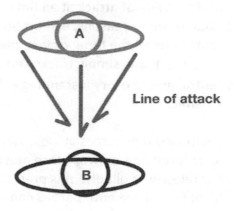

Line of attack

Figure 2.5A, both parties are within each other's line of attack.

Figure 2.5B, the opponent's line of fire is off, while one's line of attack is targeting the opponent's center axis.

Closing in

Closing in, or entering, (入身, 埋身) is a skill which is a critical for Wing Chun Kuen, which determines the successful outcome of its application. Closing in is not just to getting close to the opponent's body. Closing in is implementing the following two actions concurrently:

1) Seizing the opponent's foot position; this is to disrupt the opponent's center of gravity, cause the opponent's to be unbalanced, cause the opponent unable to retreat, or cause the opponent to not be able to proceed. A general position is such as the place behind the lead or back leg in figure 2.6.

2) Seizing the opponent's hand position; this is to avert the lead hand (as in figure 2.6) to avoid head-on confrontation or power struggle; and to control the rear hand, such as jamming it, or putting it in an awkward position for safety, and making use of the opponent's action.

In general, it is a common practice that one holds one's structure to resist, push, withstand, or to overpower the situation. This practice causes one to be unable to close in; instead, these tactics serve to utilize power or use speed in struggling at Long Fist range, or be outside the Short Strike range. Thus, one can never properly close in.

Closing in is a critical Wing Chun Kuen skill which has to be developed; it needs to become second nature for the Wing Chun Kuen practitioner. As the ancient Short Strike writings state, "Long coming, short receiving, habitually close in" (長來短接慣入身) and "Accept the incoming, escort what is leaving, disengage thrust forward" (來留去送脱手直衝), Closing in has to become a habit or second nature in order for Wing Chun Kuen to work; and one needs to know what, why, and how to thrust forward or close in.

Furthermore, in order to close in, one needs the support of a flexible physical body, footwork, and proper Wing Chun Kuen technique. Thus, one needs to have a good handling of them.

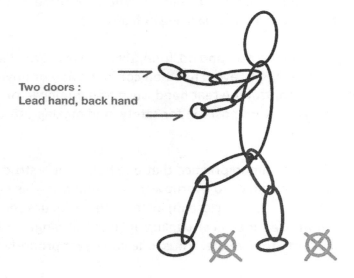

Two doors :
Lead hand, back hand

Two positions:

Behind the lead leg, behind the back leg

Figure 2.6

Receiving

Receiving is a critical method for Wing Chun Kuen. To receive, one needs to know where or which part of the opponent's body to receive, what type of receiving technique is used, and the type of body needed for receiving.

To be able to receive, the body needs to be having a characteristic similar to a coiled spring or rattan stick, which can absorb the force of the incoming object; instead of a brick wall type of body, which collides against the incoming object. Receiving is to receive the incoming attack, instead of blocking, countering, or deflecting the incoming attack.

Wing Chun Kuen moves forward at an angle to receive while concurrently closing in; Wing Chun Kuen does not move back. Wing Chun Kuen does not stand in the same fixed location, and Wing Chun Kuen does not step away and then return with two steps.

There are four basic Wing Chun Kuen techniques which are used for receiving. These are *Tan, Fuk, Bong,* and *Kei*, as shown in the following pictures.

As in figure 2.7A, *Tan* (攤) is unwrapping. In figure 2.7B, *Fuk* (覆) means cover, *Fuk* here is different from the common character in modern Wing Chun Kuen called *Fuk* (伏 to subdue). The *Yik Kam Siu Lin Tau Kuen Kuit* of 1840 recorded, "*Tan* and *Fuk* hide within silence" (攤覆靜中藏).

Figure 2.7C, shows Bong (膀). Figure 2.7D shows Kei (企); these are receiving methods which are suitable for different parts of body. The *Yik Kam Siu Lin Tau* of 1840 describes these techniques as, "Wing elbow twisting waist visit the under the flow" (膀肘拗腰流下訪), and "Erect elbow guards the chest area" (企肘護心旁).

Figure 2.7A

Figure 2.7B

Figure 2.7C

Figure 2.7D

In order to know which part of the opponent's body to be received, in Chinese martial arts, there are three passes. The three gates are the wrist or first gate, elbow or second gate, and shoulder or third gate. This is in the following figure 2.7E.

In the Short Strike art, at closing in, one does not run into the line of attack of either the lead and or the rear hand. Ideally, one receives the part of the opponent's arm, between the elbow and shoulder or beyond. As shown in figure 2.7F is the implementation of the Wing Chun Kuen saying, "Hand enters the three gates" (手入三关).

Receiving the part above elbow pass is the place to receive for the sake of one's safety and executing effective Wing Chun Kuen techniques.

Finally, the arms of Wing Chun Kuen Wooden Dummy is meant to represent the part between the elbow and shoulder; this is to bring the Wooden Dummy practice in accord to receiving and closing in the Short Strike art.

Three gates:

Wrist , Elbow, Shoulder

Figure 2.7E

Figure 2.7F

The Ancient circle platform of Chi Sau practice is the main training for practicing the receiving and closing in of Wing Chun Kuen, the following figures show the Outward Circle *Ngoi Lien Sao*, and inward circle or *Noi Liem Sao* in Chi Sau practice.

Figure 2.7F

Figure 2.7G

Footwork

Footwork is a critical element for the Sticking body Short Strike art. The implementation of receiving and closing in rely on footwork. Figure 2.8A presents a typical receiving and closing in execution; one proceeds from Position X to Position Z; with Position Y, one further closes into the body to body sticking range, which in general, is the elbow, shoulder or takedown range.

Figure 2.8 A

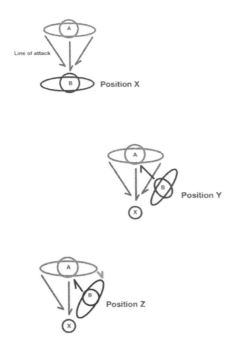

The following are two examples of the Short Strike art, these are the two fundamental footwork methods; these include: 1) Closing in from outside angle, and 2) Closing in from the inside angle.

Figure 2.8B shows the footwork of Closing in from outside angle. This example is accord to the 1700's writing, "Outward wrapping strike in searching within the chest"(外裹打入窩裡尋).

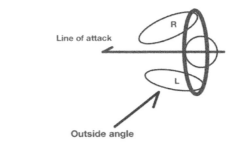

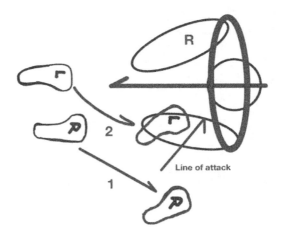

Outside angle close in foot work

Figure 2.8B

Figure 2.8C is a Wing Chun Kuen implementation of this footwork within the wooden dummy set.

Figure 2.8C

Figure 2.8D shows the footwork of the close in from in side angle. This example is accord to the 1700's writing , "Inward wrapping opens up the left and right corner" (里裏打開左右角).

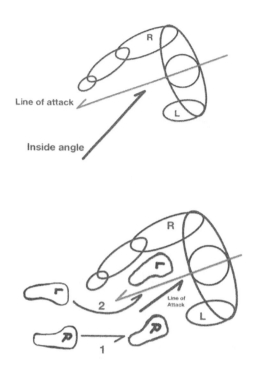

Inside angle close in foot work

Figure 2.8D

Figure 2.8E is a Wing Chun Kuen implementation of the above example with the Wooden Dummy. In this example, while closing in, one needs to stay away from the left arm or the back arm, one must not walk into the line of attack of the left arm. An alternative of handling the back arm is to jam it or disarm it.

Figure 2.8E

Figure 2.8F are the four basic types of step. These four basic steps are used to create different footwork as needed to support different variation of receiving and closing in.

Four basic step type

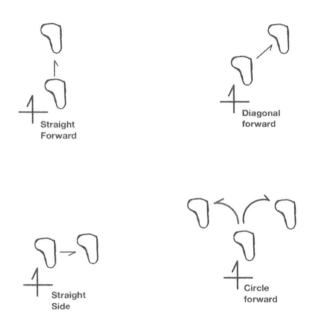

Straight Forward

Diagonal forward

Straight Side

Circle forward

Figure 2.8F

Figure 2.8G presents the ancient Short Strike footwork, these are the "Z step" and "triangle step" are commonly practiced in Wing Chun Kuen sets.

Ancient Short strike art footwork

Z step   **Triangle step**

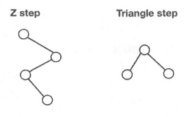

Plum flower step

Figure 2.8G

Chapter Three - Flexible physical body

PURIFY THE FIVE EYES; ATTAIN THE FIVE POWERS,
SIMPLY ACCOMPLISH THEM AND KNOW WHAT'S HARD TO FATHOM,

SHAPES IN A MIRROR ARE NOT HARD TO SEE,
BUT THE MOON IN THE WATER--HOW CAN ONE PLUCK IT OUT?

The Song of Enlightenment

In order to implement the art of Wing Chun Kuen as described in the Wing Chun Kuen *Kuit*, "Accept the incoming, escort what is leaving, disengage, thrust forward" (来留去送脱手直衝), or "Receive, stick to, close in to the opponent's body concurrently", one needs a flexible body to do it. This type of flexible body has many names such as the "rattan body", the "willow body", the "snake body", or the "dynamic seven bows body". All of these suggest flexibility with the torso.

Figure 3.1 shows the implementation of Wing Chun Kuen's Sticking to the Body Short Strike with a flexible physical body is modeled by a coiled spring; notice that a spring receives the incoming force with the side edge. This way of handling makes it possible to receive incoming force while slipping in, or closing in at an angle, without having to take collision or impact head on.

This is different from taking incoming force head on where the spring is held fixed; and limited to breaking down if the incoming force is greater than the spring coils' load limitations.

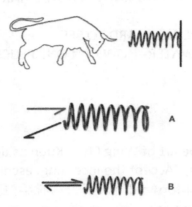

Figure 3.1, Flexible physical body model

As illustrated above, it is clear that a fixed structure, like a tripod, as shown in figure 3.2 cannot do the job; as it is set up to push the incoming object away while sitting stationary; those are the characteristics of a hard resisting Long Fist, instead of the soft Sticking to the Body Short Strike Wing Chun Kuen.

Figure 3.2 - A tripod structure physical body

In order to have this Wing Chun Kuen type of flexible physical body, one needs to have good handling of the body's major joints and the *musculo-tendon* system, which we refer to as the Seven Bows under a balanced central axis condition as in figure 3.3.

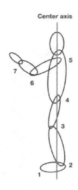

Figure 3.3, The Seven Bows and Center Axis

The seven bows are the feet bow, ankle bow, knee bow, hip bow, shoulder bow, elbow bow, and wrist bow. Only when one has good handling on these seven bows, one can have a flexible body which can implement the Wing Chun Kuen Short Strike art.

The lower four bows or the feet, ankle, knee, and hip bow are critical. Unaware of the four lower bows, or holding these four bows rigid, is a common problem of Wing Chun Kuen, and will lead to a fixed tripod structure as in figure 3.4. The inability to have flexible four lower bows will lead to inability to implement the Sticking to the Body Short Strike of Wing Chun Kuen.

The other critical element of Wing Chun Kuen flexible physical body development and handling is the handling of the center axis. At all times, the center axis needs to be handled in a balance state, or a proper physical body within centered state (正身子午). An off balanced center axis means losing the torque advantage, which is a disaster in the execution of Wing Chun Kuen Sticking to the Body Short Strike techniques.

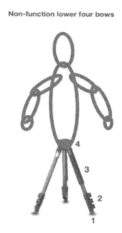

Figure 3.4, a non-functioning physical body

The *Yee Ji Kim Yeung Ma* (YJKYM) or "Parallel Clamping Yang" stance, also known as the "Equal shoulder width stance" is for the development of the Wing Chun Kuen flexible physical body. Figure 3.5 shows the five key points which is the core of the flexible physical body development; following these details that describe the five key points. In depth body development needs my 6 13 3 platform which is presented in my book, *"Basic Ancient Wing Chun Kuen Art and Science"*.

The five critical keys

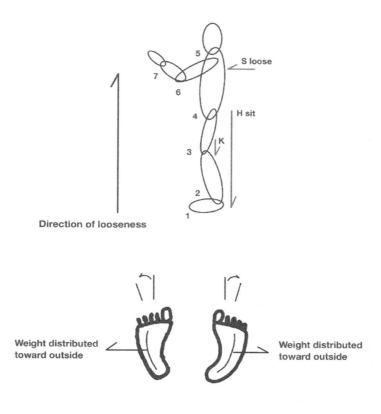

Figure 3.5, the five critical keys for flexible physical body development.

Feet Bow

As in the figure 3.5, feet bow is the first bow. This bow is extremely important because it is the interface between the physical body and the earth. As in the name YJKYM, *"Kim Yeung"* refers to placing the body weight distributed towards the outside edges of the bottom of the feet. The two big toes are either pointing straight forward or slightly tilted forward and outwards. The goal of this arrangement is to have natural, loose, and lively foot placement which supports the physical body's other six bows, without causing any one bow to be rigid. Proper foot bow handling will feel loose, light, effortless, and firmly coupled to the ground like a suction cup or spring coil supporting every part of the body, with the arches as the center of the bottom of the feet. There is no imbalance or rigid high stress point on the bottom of the feet.

Sequence of loosening

The proper sequence to loosen the body is to loosen the bows from ground up as shown in the figure 3.5. Loosening the Seven Bows with this sequence causes the bows to support each other effortlessly from the bottom up. However, wrong sequencing of loosening the body from top down will cause the bows to experience stress and cause tensing up.

For example, loosening the body with the top down sequence will cause the feet bow to step hard onto the surface of the ground; at the same time, the feet bow needs to compensate for the reaction force created by the body weight pushing into the ground, this causes the feet bow to be unable to relax and be loose; instead it will be tense and rigid.

Knee Bow

The handling of the Knee Bow is with the back of the knee – the popliteal fossa. Instead of stressing or tensing the knee cap, which can cause damage with long term wear and tear of the knee. A properly handled Knee Bow feels loose and comfortable, instead of rigid stress, as when internally rotating and fixed bending the knee as in today's Wing Chun Kuen practices.

Hip Bow

Hip Bow consists of two parts, these are the hip joints and the lower part of the spine.

The Hip Bow needs to be open, loose, as if one is "sitting down", as in figure 3.6C. A good way to experience a proper hip bow handling is to sit on a chair, with legs shoulder width, as in figure 3.6D. One can sit on a chair to experience the open, loose, and sitting down feeling of the hip joint, which can be then used as a reference for the hip bow handling while standing.

Improper Hip Bow handling is like figure 3.6B, where the buttocks pop backward, or figure 3.6A, where the tail bone is tilted forward.

Improper Hip Bow handling causes the body to break into two parts - one part above the hip, and the other part from the hip downward. This cause the top and bottom of the physical body to not mutually support each other well. Also, the improper handling of the Hip Bow causes one's breathing to be shallow, as in chest breathing, or forceful. This would be in lieu of natural effortless deep low abdominal breathing. Furthermore, the diaphragm will not be able move naturally in large amplitude to massage the internal organs and provide abundant blood circulation.

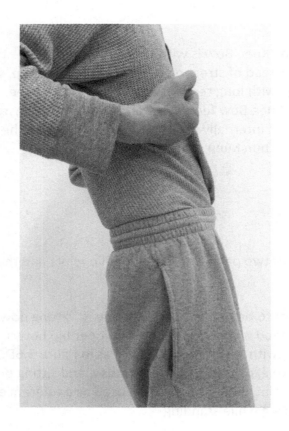

Figure 3.6A - Improper handling of Hip Bow by tucking the tailbone forward.

Figure 3.6B - Improper handling of Hip Bow by popping out the buttocks.

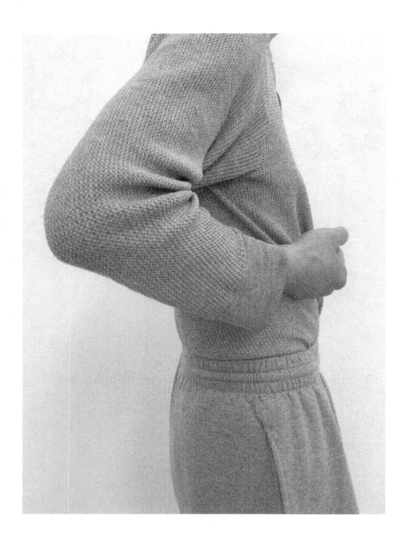

Figure 3.6C - Proper handling of Hip Bow.

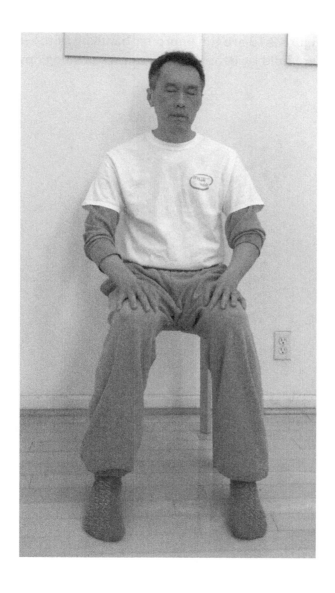

Figure 3.6D - Sitting to experience proper Hip Bow handling

In Figure 3.7C, one can see a proper handling of the lower four bows from feet bow to hip bow which get a result of effortless, naturally stable, well coupled to the ground, and spring-like coil while handling force.

Figure 3.7A and Figure 3.7B are the improper handling of the lower four bows which are hold rigid, as a tripod, or rack pushing upward from the ground.

Figure 3.7A - Improper stance handling with holding the lower four bows

Figure 3.7B - Improper handling of the stance by straightening the lower body joints

Figure 3.7C - Proper stance handling

Shoulder Bow

Shoulder Bow consists of the shoulder joints and the shoulder blade. Proper handling of the Shoulder Bow is makes it possible for effective strength transfer from the lower four bows to the fingers. Improper Shoulder Bow handling will cause one's breathing to be shallow, with the diaphragm unable to naturally function to breathe deeply and promote health. The handling of shoulder is done by slightly rolling back of the shoulder joints, with the shoulder and shoulder blade loose.

Figure 3.8A shows improper handling of Shoulder Bow where the shoulder is rolled forward and the shoulder blade pushes backward. This causes strength to be unable to travel down to the lower Bows and shallow or forceful breathing. It is known in Traditional Chinese Internal arts that this type of improper practice causes the Qi in the Lung Channel to be sluggish due to closing down of the upper chest. Long term practice of this improper way will cause the Lungs to be sluggish, Kidney Qi deficient, and weak Liver Qi circulation. The outcome will be depression, fear, and bad temper, or having inappropriate aggressiveness.

Figure 3.8B is another common improper shoulder bow handling tensing the shoulder and chest. This, too, will cause shallow or short breathing and poor chest, lung, and/or heart blood circulation.

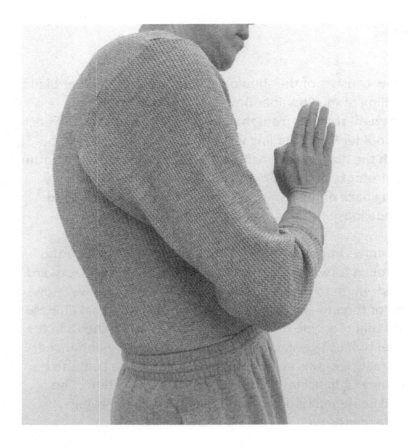

Fig 3.8A - Improper shoulder bow handling with the shoulder blade pushed out or "winging".

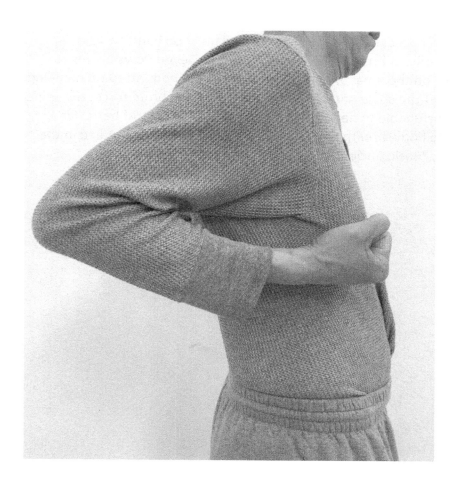

Figure 3.8B - Improper handling of shoulder bow with tense upper body.

Notice that the spine is not included in the Seven Bows diagrams. This is because the spine is fragile and must be handled with care and without brute force. Focusing on the Seven Bows means to focus on the areas which are the core of the body strength handling, and let the spine naturally align itself. If using brute force, the spine will be unable to handle the core properly. Details of basic handling of the body, breathing, strength, and Qi flow can be studied in the book, "Basic Ancient Wing Chun Kuen Art and Science".

Chapter Four - Wooden Dummy

WHO IS WITHOUT THOUGHT? WHO IS WITHOUT BIRTH?
IF THERE IS REALLY NO PRODUCTION, THERE IS NOTHING NOT PRODUCED.
SUMMON A WODDEN DUMMY AND INQUIRE OF IT.
APPLY YOURSELF TO SEEKING BUDDHAHOOD; SOONER OR LATER YOU WILL
ACCOMPLISH IT.

- Song of Enlightment

The Wing Chun wooden dummy is a learning tool, experimenting tool, or laboratory, for the serious Wing Chun Kuen practitioner. It is no different than a personal computer, or musical instrument, one uses. The Wing Chun Kuen Wooden Dummy is not an object to perform unrealistic rituals on, or mimic other sets or postures for entertainment purposes. But rather, a close partner to accompany one in the life long journey of studying Wing Chun Kuen and refining one's Wing Chun skill. As it is said in the ancient Wing Chun Kuen saying, "When there is no teacher or partner available, experiment and refine skill with the mirror and the wooden dummy" (無師無對手, 鏡與樁中求).

The following five rules are the key for proper wooden dummy practice to develop Wing Chun Kuen skill.

來留去送
脫手直衝

**Come accept leave escort
Disengage thrust forward**

Rule 1

**Make use of momentum and
tendency.**

**Avoid senseless brute force
over power.**

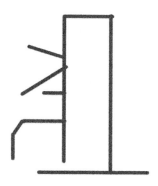

來留去送
脫手直衝

Come accept leave escort
Disengage thrust forward

Rule 1

Make use of momentum and tendency

Avoid senseless brute force and overpowering

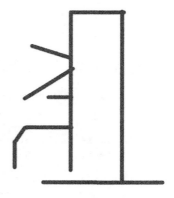

來留去送
脫手直衝

Come accept leave escort
Disengage thrust forward

Rule 2

Use flexible physical body to flow

Avoid holding structure to push
and to collide

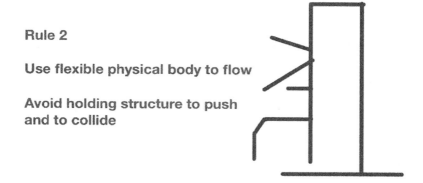

長來短接貫入身

**Long come short receive
Naturally close in**

Rule 3

Close in

Avoid staying at a distance

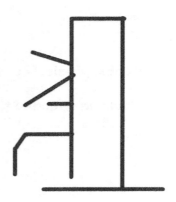

長來短接貫入身

Long come short receive
Naturally close in

Rule 4

Retract arm

**Avoid extending the arm
which loses mechanical
advantage**

自頂至足
節轉輪防

From top of the head
To bottom of the feet
Joints turn spin to guard

Rule 5

Keep center axis vertically
balanced

Avoid leaning to any direction
to cause losing of torque ability
and discontinuity within operation

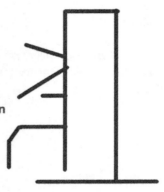

Chapter Five - Technique

"WRONG" IS NOT WRONG; "RIGHT" IS NOT RIGHT.
ERRING BY A HAIR'S BREADTH, ONE MISSES BY A THOUSAND MILES.
"RIGHT" WAS THE DRAGON-MAIDEN'S SUCCENLY ACHIEVING
BUDDHAHOOD;
"WRONG" WAS GOOD STAR'S SINKING AND FALLING WHILE ALIVE.

- Song of Enlightenment

Wing Chun Kuen techniques are well designed and calculated moves. Even though there is no perfection or ideal in real life execution of any techniques, every Wing Chun Kuen technique is based on the Sticking to the Body Short Strike components which have been presented in the previous chapters.

Figure 5.1 is an example of a proper *Tan Da* execution. Notice that when Trish executes the *Tan Da* based on the line of attack, closes in, receives, uses footwork, power generation, and proper Wing Chun Kuen mechanics.

Figure 5.1A shows the footwork supporting the line of attack, receiving, and closing in. Furthermore, as in the Figure 5.1, Trish's *Tan Sau* is changing into a strike to the center axis, head area of Jack.

Figure 5.1 - a proper *Tan Da*

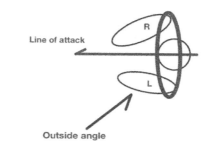

Line of attack

Outside angle

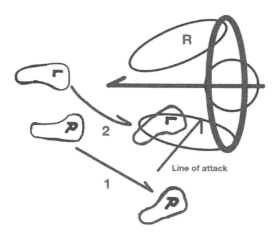

Line of attack

Outside angle close in foot work

Figure 5.1A - The proper footwork supporting the proper *Tan Da*

Figure 5.2 shows an improper *Tan Da*. This execution is problematic due to Trish positioned in the line of attack of Jack; even the *Tan Sau* obstructs Jack's arm in elbow area, Jack still can strike Trish head on. Also, this is a Long Fist method in which is pushing the opponent away instead of Sticking to the Body Short Strike method, which is closing in and receiving; as such, without the Wing Chun Kuen mechanical and torque advantage, Trish would have a disadvantage facing Jack. The outcome of Trish facing a stronger Jack is predictable.

Figure 5.2 - An improper *Tan Da*

Figure 5.3 is another improper execution of Wing Chun *Tan Da*. It is a Long Fist method without the Wing Chun mechanics advantage, and the *Tan Sau* obstruction at the wrist gate is not effective, and in fact, a wasted move, because it doesn't influence Jack's attack much. Jack's next strike will strike Trish's center axis heavily.

Figure 5.3- Another improper *Tan Da*

From these improper Tan Da examples above, even though one they all might be view as applying the Wing Chun cancel and strike in the same time (連消帶打) concept; however, failing to apply the rule of game of the strict body Short Strike of Wing Chun Kuen causes disaster.

Figure 5.4 a proper outside angle lap Ta , close in and receive at the third gate.

Figure 5.4A - A proper inside angle *Lap Da*, closing in and receiving at the third gate.

Figure 5.4 and Figure 5.4A show proper *Lap Da* execution. Figure 5.5 shows proper elbow strikes to the chest with the consideration to avoid the hook; Wing Chun mechanics is applied here; using less effort to handle the strong opponent.

Figure 5.5 - a proper inside angle elbow

Chapter Six -Beginning of the Journey

If someone is surrounded by vicious bandits,
Who threaten him with knives,
If he evokes the strength of Avalokitesvara,
The bandits will all give rise to compassion.

- Lotus Sutra

Wing Chun Kuen is a well design martial technology. There is no myth or secret, as it is scientific. As a science, it is repeatable and with quality results. Mind power, Qi power, *Jin*, Internal Art labels, and all kinds of philosophical beliefs can never replace the Wing Chun Kuen technology. Unless one studies Wing Chun Kuen technology, one never knows what it is how it is done, and why it is done as such. Thus, one simply doesn't know and cannot develop Wing Chun Kuen.

However, no technology can replace continuous practice and refinement. Kung Fu comes from properly learning the Wing Chun Kuen basics and continually refining in action, not through speculation.

As in ancient traditional Chinese martial art, Wing Chun Kuen has two parts, these are: 1) the body of the art, and 2) the application of the art. The chapter of the flexible physical body is a presentation of the body of the art. The rest of the chapters in this book present the application of the art. The body of the art is the basis of application of the art. Without good development of the body of the art, one will not be able to reach a deeper level of handling the application of the art. Also, as in the chapter of flexible physical body, the development of the body of the art influences health. Thus, one has to have a proper and balanced practice in order to get the results of strengthening the body and ability for self-defense. The details of proper and balanced practice according to ancient Wing Chun Kuen can be found in the book, "Basic Ancient Wing Chun Kuen Art and Science" by Hendrik Santo.

To learn and develop the proper technology of Wing Chun Kuen is needed in order to get the result of strengthening the body and self-defense; however, it is equally important to live a proper life that contributes positively and constructively to oneself and society.

Finally, to start the journey of Wing Chun Kuen, since Wing Chun Kuen is a Buddhist art, the following are the rules of martial arts practice according the ancient Buddhist Shaolin school. For thousands of years, these are proven good principles to follow, to result in a good respectable living, and avoid causing unnecessary trouble.

1. To study martial art, one must place strengthening the body and mind as the first priority, thus, one must practice day and night diligently. (习武者，以强健体魄为要旨，宜朝夕行事，不可随意作辍)

2. Following the teaching of the Buddha, one must practice compassion towards every living being. Even if one has accomplished advanced skill, one must use the skill for self-defense only; one must avoid fighting or testing one's skill to prove who is the best fighter or number one. Violation of these is taken as the breaking the Law. (宜入佛门，悲怜为怀，纵于技术精娴，只可习以自卫，切戒逞气血之私，好勇斗狠，犯者与违反朝规同罪)

3. One must behave, and be kind and honest, taking good care of one's parents, and never bullying others with one's skill.
温良、诚信，孝双亲，不得恃强凌弱，任意妄为。

To conclude this book, the following checklist is needed for the beginning of the Wing Chun Kuen journey:

Basic Wing Chun Kuen Skill Check List

_____ Line of Attack
_____ Close in
_____ Receive
_____ Footwork
_____ Technique

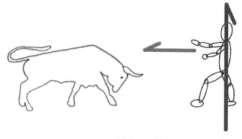

_____ Wing Chun mechanics
_____ Wing Chun power generation
_____ Flexible Physical body

iYikKam platform

About the Author:

Hendrik Santo, MScEE, is a power management semiconductor design architect based in the Silicon Valley California. He is a 40 year researcher of Wing Chun Kuen, and more than 20 years research in the Six Healing Sounds. He is also a grand student of Grandmaster Ma Li Tang of the Six Healing Sounds. He was a student of the Chan Patriarch, the late Venerable Master Hsuan Hua.

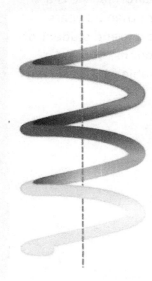

咏春 6.13.3

Made in United States
North Haven, CT
21 June 2024

53901223R00059